Berlin Schöneweide yards, rebuilt Kriegslok (Austerity loco) 2-10-0 no 52 8100-1 is waiting to leave tender first with a local trip freight while a Russian built class 120 Co-Co diesel electric looks on.

1

2 A view of the coaling facility and yard at Berlin Schöneweide loco depot. Two class 52 Kriegsloks have been rebuilt for use as stationary boilers.

Unrebuilt class 52 Kriegslok 2-10-0s at Berlin Schöneweide . A Berlin electric suburban train passes behind.

4 Light standard pacific, 03 2128-1, still fitted with the original type boiler, backs towards the turntable at Berlin Schöneweide roundhouse. The depot had an allocation of Kriegsloks which were mainly used on trip freights around Berlin, but locos, both passenger and freight, visited frequently for servicing from other depots.

Pacific 03 2128-1 being turned.

6 2128-1 has now been turned and backs off the turntable.

2128-1 moves over to the waiting lines ready to take a rush hour train to Gorlitz from Schöneweide station.

8 An overall view of Schöneweide roundhouse, 03 2128-1 has just been turned, and three Kriegsloks, 52 1564, rebuilt 52 8181 and an unidentified sister fitted with a Giesl ejector, are awaiting their next duties.

Oil fired class 50-35 2-10-0 no 50 0035-1 has worked into Berlin on a freight train from the North. Having been serviced at Schöneweide depot, she is awaiting time to return home with a tank train.

10 Unrebuilt class 52 Kriegslok no 52 1564-5 awaiting her next duty at Schöneweide depot. Behind is a rebuilt sister of class 52-8.

A withdrawn class 01 standard heavy pacific in the roundhouse at Schöneweide.

12　Class 50-35 2-10-0 50 3707-2 pulls into Halberstadt yards with a mixed freight.

3707-2 has uncoupled her train and now heads for the loco depot.

One of the last unrebuilt class 01 heavy pacifics, 01 2137-6 at Halberstadt depot.

Oil fired metre gauge 2-10-2 tank 99 0235-4 pulls into Wernigerode Westerntor station with a train for Nordhausen on the Harzquerbahn.

2-10-2T 99 0245-3 waits to leave Drei Annen Höhne with a Wernigerode train. This was the junction for the line to the Brocken summit, which at the time was only open for public trains as far as Scheirke.

Metre gauge trains passing at Benneckenstein, both hauled by oil fired 2-10-2 tanks.

18 A general view of Nordhausen metre gauge station; 99 0235-4 having arrived from Wernigerode has pushed her train back and run round.

0235-4 shunting stock at Nordhausen.

0235-4 waits to leave Nordhausen with a train for Wernigerode.

44 0635-1, an oil fired standard 3 cylinder 2-10-0 runs light engine tender first through Nordhausen station. Interestingly, sister 44 636 was allocated to Rheine depot on the DB in West Germany.

3 cylinder 2-10-0 44 0651-4 of Saalfeld depot waits to leave Gera with a freight train.

Glauchau was the last depot with an allocation of class 58-3. These were 3 cylinder 2-10-0s rebuilt by DR from Prussian G-12s. The rebuild included 3 sets of Walschaerts valve gear instead of the original conjugated gear and a welded boiler. 58 3028-6 is waiting to head east from Glauchau with a train of bogie mineral wagons.

24 Another view of 58 3028-6 at Glauchau station.

Another class 58-3, stored minus number plates, seen from a passing train at Glauchau loco depot.

Rebuilt "Kriegslok" 52 8019-3 on a mixed freight train near Dresden Neustadt.

760mm gauge 2-10-2 tank loco 99 1757-6 waits to leave Zittau, close to the Czechoslovakian and Polish borders, with a train for Kurort Jonsdorf. At the time, Zittau depot still had an allocation of class 52-8 2-10-0s and played regular host to CSD class 556 2-10-0s but photography on the standard gauge station there was not permitted due to its border status.

28 760mm gauge 2-10-2T 99 1760-1 waits to leave Bertsdorf with a train for Kurort Oybin. Bertsdorf was the junction where the line from Zittau split into two branches to Kurort Jonsdorf and Kurort Oybin.

Saalfeld was the place where the last great steam show in Germany was played out. A road bridge over the northern station throat was an excellent vantage point to observe operations and the locomotive depot. The authorities understood the attraction and lifted the normal restriction forbidding photographing railways from bridges here.

A busy scene at Saalfeld Depot, 3 cylinder 2-10-0 44 0280-6 passes light engine as a sister moves onto the turntable.

Saalfeld Depot, 44 0280-6 runs past as a sister is turned and a class 41 coal fired 2-8-2 and class 01-5 Pacific await their call to duty.

32 Another view from the road bridge at Saalfeld, 44 0413-3 crosses the station throat light engine. These powerful locomotives were nick-named "Jumbos" by the German railwaymen.

With drain cocks open, 44 0601-3 prepares to tackle the climb on the line towards Gera with a mineral train at Saalfeld.

2-10-0 44 0689-8 runs into Saalfeld with a mixed freight train from the Jena line.

50 3565-4 in ex works condition at Halberstadt depot.

50 3017-9 at Glauchau. This loco retained her Prussian tender.

36 0025-7 has been given permission by the signalman and proceeds back to the south end of the station. Behind, Class 44 2-10-0s await their next duties.

Oil fired class 01-5 Pacific 01 0520-5 runs light past Saalfeld roundhouse. These locos were rebuilt from standard 01 Pacifics by DR's Meiningen works in the early 1960s

Oil fired 2-10-2 tank loco 95 0028-1, an ex- Prussian class T20, waits to leave Saalfeld with a passenger train for Sonneberg. These huge locomotives survived at Probstzella depot for working this steeply graded line until the end of 1980. The loco's right side cylinder cover has fallen off and been placed in front of the smokebox.

2-10-2T 95 0025-7 has arrived at Saalfeld with a train from Sonneberg and run forward. She stands behind the "W" await instructions board before heading back across the layout.

2-10-0 44 0567-6 takes water on the goods line next to Saalfeld station.

40 In 1981 the metre gauge Selketalbahn in the Harz was still not connected to the Harzquerbahn. 0-4-4-0 Mallet tank loco 99 5906-5 takes water at Alexisbad before taking her train to Gernrode.

In 1981, trains from Gernrode terminated at Straßberg. The unique 2-6-2 Tank 99 6001-4 has run around her train which is waiting to depart for Alexisbad.

Another 0-4-4-0T number 99 5902-4 attacks the steeply graded branch to Harzgerode out of Alexisbad.

6001-4 takes water at Alexisbad.

Alexisbad, 99 6001-4 has arrived from Straßberg and runs around her train which she will take up the branch line to Harzgerode. This locomotive was built by Krupp as a prototype in 1939, but no further examples were built due to the Second World War.

6001-4 waits to depart Harzgerode with a train to Gernrode.

On the "Nebenbahn" (secondary line) from Vitzenberg to Querfurt, rebuilt Kriegslok 52 8077-1 of Roblingen depot, pauses at a wayside station with a short train comprising of a four wheeled parcels brake van and two six wheeled coaches.

8077-1 running tender first with a Vitzenburg to Querfurt train, is waiting for a diesel hauled train to pass at a wayside station. This line was closed to passengers in 1998 and to all traffic in 2003.

The class 110 diesel hauled train to Vitzenburg has passed comprising 6x 6 wheeled coaches with loco 110 140-1, and 52 8077-1 is clear to depart for Querfurt. Full dieselization of the line was imminent.

Röblingen depot, rebuilt Kriegslok 2-10-0 52 8063-1 and a sister await their call to duty.

At Cranzahl in the Iron Mountains, a 760mm gauge 2-10-2 tank loco has been loaded onto a standard gauge transporter wagon and awaits transport to Gorlitz works.

760mm gauge 2-10-2T 99 1775-8 in pristine condition waits to leave Cranzahl with a train for the ski resort of Kurort Oberwiesental on the Czechoslovakian border.

The narrow gauge station at Cranzahl could use a coat of paint! 2-10-2T 99 1775-8 awaits the arrival of the connecting standard gauge train before tackling the steeply graded line to Kurort Oberwiesental.

A 2-10-2T with a Cranzahl bound train approaches the station at Kretscham-Rothensehma in falling snow.

760mm gauge Saxon class IVk 0-4-4-0 Meyer articulated tank loco number 99 1590-1 stands out of use outside Johstadt depot.

0-4-4-0T 99 1561-2 in steam at Johstadt depot with nothing to do. Her train had been replaced by a bus.

1561-2 is seen taking water at Wolkenstein loco shed. On the adjacent track is a transporter wagon for carrying standard gauge wagons.

Another Saxon Meyer, 99 1585-1, is being coaled at Wolkenstein.

1585-1 is serviced at Johstadt after the run from Wolkenstein.

Rebuilt oil fired pacific 01 0517-1 at Saalfeld. This was the last of this class of loco to retain her original conical smokebox door. As rebuilt, these semi-streamlined locos also featured deep skirts on the running plate and some had boxpok driving wheels.

A class 44 three cylinder 2-10-0 powers up the climb away from Saalfeld with a mixed freight train for Gera.

Pacific 01 0517-1 is turned on Saalfeld turntable. The diesels at the roundhouse are the recently delivered Romanian built class 119 Co-Co diesel electrics. These proved troublesome in their early days, which probably accounted for Saalfeld depot's continued use of the Pacifics.

Saalfeld's 01-5 Pacific 01 0524-7 waits to leave Leipzig Hauptbahnhof (main station) with a stopping train for Saalfeld.

60 0524-7's train consists of a goods van and 6x 6 wheeled coaches, hardly a taxing load for the Pacific. At the time, these were the last regular steam workings into Leipzig's magnificent station.